In the War

Evacuation

Simon Adams

First published in 2008 by Wayland

Copyright © Wayland 2008

This paperback edition published in 2010 by Wayland

Wayland
338 Euston Road
London NW1 3BH

Wayland Australia
Level 17/207 Kent Street
Sydney, NSW 2000

Editor: Camilla Lloyd
Designer: Phipps Design
Picture researcher: Shelley Noronha

Acknowledgments:
The publishers would like to thank Pamela Daymond and the trustees of the Imperial War Museum for their kind permission to quote from personal letters, (p.22-23).

Picture Acknowledgments: The author and publisher would like to thank the following for their pictures to be reproduced in this publication: Cover photographs: Wayland Picture Library (both); Corbis: 26, © Hulton-Deutsch Collection/Corbis: 1, 4, 7, 9, 11, 14, 15, 20, 23, 25, 29; Imperial War Museum/ref HU69022: 21; HIP/The Lordprice Collection/ Topfoto: 24, Roger-Viollet/Topfoto: 12, TIP/Jewish Chronicle Archive/Topfoto: 8, Topfoto: 5, 10, 16, 18, 23, 27, 28; Wayland Picture Library: 13, 17, 19.

British Library Cataloguing in Publication Data:
Adams, Simon, 1955-
    Evacuation. - (In the war)
    1. World War, 1939-1945 - Evacuation of civilians - Great Britain - Juvenile literature
    2. World War, 1939-1945 - Children - Great Britain - Juvenile literature
    3. World War, 1939-1945 - Social aspects - Great Britain – Juvenile literature
    I. Title
    940.5'3161

ISBN: 978 0 7502 6161 6

Printed in China

Wayland is a division of Hachette Children's Books, an Hachette UK company
www.hachette.co.uk

Contents

World War II

During World War II, hundreds of thousands of people were evacuated from their homes to escape German bombing raids on British towns and cities. The war, which broke out in September 1939, was caused by Germany's invasion of Poland. Poland's **allies**, Britain and France, then declared war on Germany. The war lasted six terrible years, with huge loss of life on both sides.

In 1918, Germany had been defeated at the end of World War I (1914–18). The peace terms it had to sign were harsh. It lost much territory and had to pay massive **compensation** to Britain, France and the other victorious allies. In 1933, Adolf Hitler and the **Nazi Party** came to power in Germany. Hitler wanted to overthrow the peace terms and make Germany a powerful nation again.

Think about
What sort of thoughts would you have had on the day war was declared?

Newspaper sellers in Piccadilly Circus in London announce the invasion of Poland on 1 September 1939 and the British preparations for war.

4

Hitler quickly built up Germany's armed services and tore up her international agreements. He took over Austria in 1938 and, later the same year, seized German-speaking border areas in Czechoslovakia, occupying the country the following year. He then turned his attention to Poland, demanding that it hand over the strip of Polish land that separated the main part of Germany from its eastern province of Prussia. When Poland refused, Germany invaded.

Although Britain then declared war on Germany, many people were reluctant to fight. They remembered the horrors of World War I and did not want to repeat them. Many people, including the prime minister, Neville Chamberlain, had hoped that Hitler might be bought off and were let down when this did not happen. No one wanted the war, and no one really knew what sort of war to expect.

In 1938, the British prime minister Neville Chamberlain hoped he had an agreement with Germany to maintain peace in Europe. Within a year, the two nations were at war.

INSIDE STORY:

'This morning the British ambassador in Berlin handed the German government a final note, stating that unless the British government heard from them by 11 o'clock that they were prepared to withdraw their troops from Poland, a state of war would exist between us. I have to tell you that no such undertaking has been received, and that consequently this country is at war with Germany.'

Prime Minister Neville Chamberlain made a radio broadcast to the British people on Sunday morning, 3 September.

Planning for evacuation

Throughout its history, Britain had been protected from invasion because it was an island. That protection ended with the invention of the aeroplane. During World War I, more than 1,400 **civilians** had been killed in German air-raids by airships and then heavy **bombers**. The biggest fear was of enemy bombers.

As early as 1924, the government's **Air-Raid Precautions (ARP)** Committee discussed the **evacuation** of civilians from the centre of London. It planned to keep essential workers in the city, but evacuate women, children, old and ill people. In 1931, another committee came up with the horrifying estimate that, on the first day of war, the enemy might drop 3,500 tonnes of **bombs** on London and other cities, causing 60,000 dead and 120,000 wounded, followed by further raids that would kill 66,000 people and injure 130,000 people each week. Faced with this possibility, it would be essential to evacuate at least 3.5 million people from London alone.

The government appealed for women volunteers to help evacuate people from towns and cities.

Think about

What thoughts would you have at the threat of a war that might destroy your house, and perhaps kill your family and friends?

Plans for evacuation still relied on people in large cities making their own arrangements with family or friends in the countryside. This changed in September 1938, when Britain almost went to war over German threats to Czechoslovakia. The government quickly published detailed evacuation plans for London, major cities such as Birmingham, Liverpool and Glasgow, and ports and naval stations such as Portsmouth, Chatham, and Rosyth in Scotland. Every household received a leaflet entitled *Evacuation – Why and How?*, explaining how evacuation would work. Lists of evacuees were drawn up, **reception areas** were planned in the countryside to receive evacuees, and rehearsals were held in London and Birmingham. The newly formed Women's Voluntary Service (**WVS**) linked up with the Girl Guides and Women's Institutes to organize the forthcoming evacuation.

INSIDE STORY:

'*A little while before war broke out, we had a sort of practice going to the school with our suitcase and gas mask and getting on the tram to go to the railway station.*'

June Cohen from Stoke Newington.

Everyone, including women and children, were issued with gas masks in case gas-filled bombs were dropped during the war.

Evacuation from Europe

The years leading up to the outbreak of World War II in 1939 were painful years for one particular group of children in Europe. For some of them, Britain became a place of **refuge**.

The Nazi government of Adolf Hitler that came to power in Germany in 1933 was strongly **anti-Semitic**, that is prejudiced against Jewish people. New laws stripped all Jews of German citizenship, forbade them to marry Germans and to teach in schools. Gangs of Nazis attacked Jews, looted their businesses and burned their synagogues.

Many Jewish families joined friends or family in Britain or elsewhere in Europe or the USA. Many more Jews left Austria after Germany took over that country in March 1938. However, although the Nazis encouraged Jews to emigrate, they took all their possessions and money so that they were left with only a suitcase of clothes. Other countries then refused to accept them because they were too poor.

INSIDE STORY:

'With a shudder the train moved forward a few yards and stopped again … Now it was the turn of the Dutch customs officials. These men had smiles on their faces and although we couldn't understand a word they said, we knew they were saying "Welcome to Holland". We all relaxed.'

Olga Drucker was 11 when she left her home in Stuttgart and came to Britain in the *Kinderstransport*.

The British government issued documents such as these to Jewish children fleeing Nazi Germany to allow them to enter Britain.

Attacks against Jews in Germany came to a head on the night of 9 November 1938. More than 7,500 Jewish shops were attacked and synagogues burned on *Kristallnacht*, the 'Night of Broken Glass'. In Britain, Jewish charities successfully urged the government to accept Jewish children up to 17 who would be brought to Britain to live with adoptive parents. The first *Kindertransport* arrived at Harwich from Germany in December 1938. From then on, two transports a week brought 9,354 Jewish children to safety. The last train left Berlin on 31 August 1939, the day before Germany invaded Poland. Many of these children never saw their parents again.

Think about
If you were a Jewish child leaving your family in Germany, would you be happy to come to Britain?

A group of Jewish children arrive in Southampton on board the US liner *Manhattan*.

The Phoney War

By the end of August 1939, it became clear that war was about to break out in Europe. On Monday 28 August 1939, children in areas to be evacuated – such as London and other large cities – were called back to school to take part in a huge evacuation rehearsal. Within days, that rehearsal became the real thing.

The German invasion of Poland on 1 September led Britain to declare war two days later. The government now issued the order to evacuate. In London 6,000 cars and buses carried more than 345,000 children to local stations to board a train out of the city; 40,000 children were evacuated from Leeds and thousands more from Birmingham, the Medway towns, Liverpool and elsewhere. In all, about 1.5 million children on their own and mothers with young children were evacuated in the first five days of September.

The evacuation generally went smoothly. No children were lost or injured and families were kept together on the journey. Most remarkably, while this was taking place, daily life went on as usual.

During the Phoney War, the government issued this poster advising mothers not to bring their children home from the countryside.

Think about

Would you want to stay away from home when there were no bombing raids and it was safe to return?

Once evacuated, the children, along with the rest of the country, waited for the bombing to begin, but nothing happened for months! People called the first seven months of the war – up to the start of April 1940 – a 'Phoney War', as fighting only took place in Eastern Europe and no bombing raids hit Britain. Parents started bringing their children home. Many children who returned home for Christmas stayed with their parents afterwards. By January 1940, more than 900,000 evacuees had returned home, including most mothers.

Some children stayed behind with their parents in London and other cities and helped out at home. This London child is helping her father dig his allotment on Hampstead Heath.

11

The big exit

In April 1940, the Phoney War ended when Germany invaded Denmark and Norway. The next month German troops swept into the Netherlands, Belgium and France. By the end of June, France had surrendered. Britain now faced Germany alone.

The German invasion of Britain was expected any day. The Battle of Britain between the Royal Air Force (**RAF**) and the German *Luftwaffe* for control of Britain's skies was fought between July and October 1940, while the first major bombing raids of the **Blitz** – the German aerial bombardment of British cities – began in September. The war was now real.

INSIDE STORY:

'I was evacuated from Dartford [Kent] on 14 June with my school. I was told by my parents the day before I was going to be evacuated. My mother told me that I was to be a good girl and that I wasn't to cry. We all queued up, we had our teeth looked at and our hair examined – prodded about for nits. Then we walked up the hill in the usual crocodile to Dartford Station, where we caught a train.'

Mavis Kerr remembers her evacuation day.

Mothers and their young children wait at Victoria Station in London to be evacuated out of the city.

Between 13–18 June, 100,000 children were moved out of London and southeast England to the West Country and Wales. Another 210,000 children were evacuated by the beginning of August. These figures include children evacuated from coastal towns that would be invaded first. Some of these children had previously been evacuated out of London, so were on the move for the second time within a year. Other evacuations took place across the country, notably from cities that had recently been bombed, such as Coventry and Hull.

In June 1940, the British-owned Channel Islands off the coast of France were threatened with German invasion. The islands were not important enough to defend from attack, so all children, mothers with children under school age and men from 20–33 who wanted to serve in the forces – a total of 36,000 people – were evacuated during the month. A further 12,000 people of all ages were evacuated by July 1941 from Gibraltar, a British colony in southern Spain. These evacuees did not see their homes again for five years.

Some children who stayed behind in London during the Blitz were made homeless when their houses were bombed.

Think about
Would you want to be evacuated to a safe place, or would you rather stay with family and friends in familiar surroundings?

Leaving home

As soon as war broke out, the Ministry of Home Defence took responsibility for organizing and coordinating evacuation. The department advised people in threatened areas to leave their homes because of the threat of bombing or invasion. Those people that took this advice did so voluntarily, for no one was ever forced to move if they did not want to.

The actual evacuation process was managed by local education authorities and schoolteachers, many of whom accompanied classes of evacuated children to their destinations. Volunteers from the WVS helped by taking children to the railway stations and looking after them during the journey.

Children in London were evacuated on the underground to outer London areas where they joined trains or boarded buses within 15 minutes of arrival. To cope with the huge numbers involved, trains ran out of London's mainline stations every nine minutes throughout the day. Large numbers of London Transport buses were used, along with trams, lorries and private cars.

Three young children – with their name labels around their necks – wait on a railway station platform to be evacuated in 1941.

Think about
If you live in a city, do you know anybody in the countryside you could go and stay with?

These five children were evacuated from London to a village in Surrey and are meeting their new family for the first time.

Alongside this publicly organized evacuation was an even bigger privately organised evacuation. Many people in the cities had friends and families who lived in the countryside whom they could live with if the bombing raids started. Some two million people organized their own evacuation in the months immediately before the war started, with many more following them in the first few months of the war. These were the lucky evacuees, for they already knew who they would be staying with, and the conditions in which they would be living.

INSIDE STORY:

'Immediately [war broke out] we were swamped by telephone requests from relations, friends (and their friends!) anxious to get away from the large cities in fear of the air-raids which were expected immediately. That evening our house contained 18 extra people; we only had five bedrooms, so all rooms except the kitchen were used; my brother and I had to sleep on the billiard table.'

Tom Dewar lived in a large house outside Callander in Perthshire during the war.

The billet

The local billeting or housing officer had the task of finding evacuees somewhere to stay. The billeting officer was appointed by the local council's housing department and was responsible for finding **billets** (temporary housing) and placing evacuees in them. The officer also had to find schools for every child.

Some people were happy to accept evacuees, but many did not want to house complete strangers. The billeting officer, therefore, sometimes had to force people to accept evacuees. Mostly, however, they used their local knowledge of who had spare rooms and if necessary used persuasion. Billeting allowances were paid to those taking evacuees at the rate of between 8s 6d (42p) and 15s (75p) a week for each unaccompanied child depending on their age. Those taking a mother and child received 5s (25p) a week for the mother and 3s (15p) per week for each child. Local doctors provided free medical care.

The government encouraged people to take in evacuees as a national service to the troops fighting abroad.

Think about
How would you feel waiting to be chosen by complete strangers to live in their house?

Thank you SAYS THE SOLDIER

to hear that you and the baby are now away safe in the country. It's grand too, to know that you are both so happy and comfortable there. Will you pleas[e] thank Mrs Ronda[...]

CARING FOR EVACUEES IS A NATIONAL SERVICE

ISSUED BY THE MINISTRY OF HEALTH

On arrival at their destination, the billeting officer took the evacuees to a central clearing point, for example the Odeon Cinema in Redhill, Surrey and the cattle market in Sevenoaks, Kent. Here the evacuees were fed and given emergency rations – a can of meat, two cans of milk and biscuits were usual – for the next two days. Quite often, however, people who had volunteered to accept evacuees came to the clearing point and picked those they would house. Some children were chosen because they were the same age as the billeter's own children, others because they were young or looked nice. However, it was often difficult to place large families, so brothers and sisters could be separated.

The billeting officer organizes billets for evacuated children as their potential families look on from the side.

Into the unknown

Some children were evacuated hundreds of miles away from their homes to a different part of the country. For them, it was like living in a foreign land.

The first problem was understanding local accents. Mavis Kerr was evacuated from London to Devon: 'Aunt May had a broad Devon accent; at first I couldn't understand a word she was saying and she couldn't understand a word I was saying.' Another problem arose when children from Liverpool and the northwest were evacuated to North Wales, where their hosts spoke only Welsh.

INSIDE STORY:

'On arrival we were met by a group of people chattering away in a foreign accent. We honestly couldn't understand a word, but I think they were offering us accommodation.'

Eddie Roland was evacuated to Glasgow

For many children, evacuation into the countryside was a huge step into the unknown.

Some children quickly picked up the language but others struggled to understand what was said to them.
Different religions proved a problem. Many Roman Catholic and Jewish children found themselves staying with Anglican or nonconformist families or in areas without a Catholic church or a synagogue. Catholic children went to strange church services, or alternated between going to the church or chapel of their hosts one Sunday and then to their own church the next. Some Jewish children went to synagogue on Saturday and then church on Sunday.

Jewish children also had problems with diet. The Chief Rabbi had broadcast early in the war that it was all right to eat pork, which was usually forbidden to Jews, but other foods were strange to their taste. All evacuated children had to get used to new food, but most soon grew to like good country cooking. Some children in Yorkshire, however, found it strange to start a meal with Yorkshire pudding and gravy and then go on to meat and vegetables!

A group of evacuated children sit down to a meal served by their new 'mother'.

Think about
How would you like to eat strange food?

Life away from home

Many children found evacuation difficult to cope with. Their new 'families' tried to make them feel comfortable and encouraged them to call the adults 'Uncle' and 'Auntie'. For many children, however, life was now completely different to the life they had led at home.

The biggest change was for children brought up in poor, cramped housing in the East End of London and other cities. Some children were used to eating their meals on the floor as there was never enough room at home to all sit down at the table. Many ate with just a knife, not a fork as well. Many more were unused to hot running water and clean toilets. They had slept two or three to a bed, or underneath the bed if there was no room in it.

Moving into the countryside was a huge shock. Many evacuees were billeted in cottages with no electricity – just oil lamps – and an outside toilet at the end of the garden. Others found themselves in larger houses with hot running water and baths, but feared they might drown in the water!

Think about
How would you like to live in a strange house without your parents?

A Devonshire farmer's wife scrubs the hair of one evacuee who has been helping to bring in the potato harvest.

They were now expected to wash every day, and had a bed of their own, and clean sheets.

The biggest shock was the countryside itself. Many children had never seen the countryside before and found it quiet and lonely. Many had also never seen a cow or a sheep in real life, and did not realise where milk, eggs or butter came from. Most adapted quickly, helping out on farms and in gardens, and learning how to catch rabbits and other skills.

INSIDE STORY:

'The cow is a mammal. It has six sides, right, left, an upper and below. At the back it has a tail, on which hangs a brush…. The horns are to butt with, and the mouth is to moo with: Under the cow hangs the milk.'

A 10-year-old evacuee from London had never seen a cow before and wrote an essay about it.

Many evacuated children had never seen a farm animal before but soon got used to their strange looks and noises.

Keeping in touch

The first job every evacuated child had to do when they settled in to their new house was to send a postcard home telling their parents where they now lived. Parents did not know where their children were going, so waited anxiously for their postcard.

From then on children sent regular letters and postcards home. They wrote about the house, their bedroom and the family they lived with. They also wrote about new friends they had made, the places they visited, and the things that happened to them everyday. Some of these letters were happy, but others were sad, for many children were lonely, and some were scared.

INSIDE STORY:

'We had a piece of sponge cake and a glass of milk before finding out why we had a postcard in our case. Our new 'Auntie' wrote her name and address on the back, and we walked to the post box to send them home, so that Mummy and Daddy would know where we were.'

Joyce Fry.

Adventures in the countryside gave children much to write home about.

One young girl, Pam, was evacuated to Exeter to escape the bombing of London, but was then bombed out in Exeter. She wrote to her parents on 4 May 1942: 'The warning sounded at 1.45 am. Soon the planes were over and bombs were dropped. Jean and I dived under the dining room table. Then Mrs Every went upstairs and shouted or rather screamed that the house was on fire. We all went up the stairs and Jean and I took turns in pumping the **stirrup pump**. . . . While we were pumping Jerry [the Germans] dropped **high explosives** and it blew the windows in. . . . Then the roof fell in and high explosives were still dropping near us. . . . We've hardly got any clothes left. . . . Mrs Every hasn't a stick left of her house except two pictures. The house is absolutely gutted. Nothing left except the four walls. Hope you are all well. See you all soon, love Pam.'

Parents sometimes came out to visit their evacuated children in the countryside and were greeted with great excitement.

Think about
What would you write in your letters home?

Evacuation overseas

A small group of evacuated children experienced a very different life from their friends. These were the children sent overseas.

In the years leading up to the war, some rich parents sent their children to live with relatives abroad. This was not an option available to poorer families. The situation changed in June 1940, when the threat of German invasion was at its height. Offers poured in from Commonwealth countries, notably Newfoundland and Canada, and from the USA. The government set up the Children's Overseas Reception Board (CORB) to evacuate children overseas; three-quarters of the children helped had to come from state schools.

Evacuated children were included in 'Goodnight Children Everywhere', a popular song written in 1939.

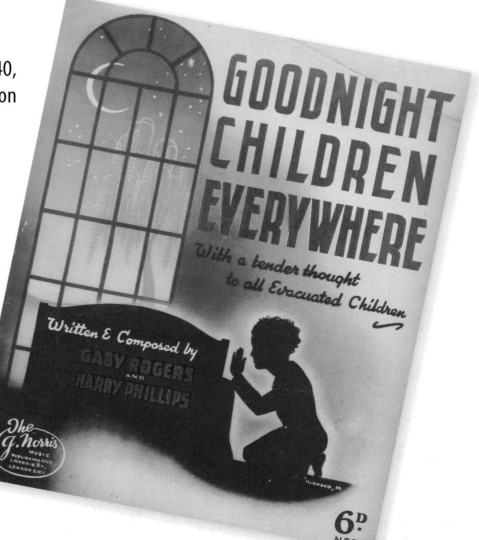

By early July, applications had been received on behalf of 200,000 children. By 15 August, 19,365 children were approved for emigration, almost all of whom came from state schools. Deciding to send your children abroad was not an easy decision, for it was unlikely you would see them again until the end of the war, and no one knew how long that would be.

The other danger was the journey itself. German U-boats (submarines) were attacking all shipping in the North Atlantic, and were unlikely to spare a ship carrying evacuees. This danger became real when the SS *Volendam* was torpedoed on 30 August 1940. Luckily, the captain managed to transfer everyone on lifeboats to other ships. Two weeks later, the SS *City of Benares* was sunk with the loss of 73 evacuees' lives. The overseas evacuation scheme was stopped with only 2,700 children moved abroad. Those children remained abroad for the rest of the war.

Think about
Would you want to be evacuated overseas or remain at home?

A group of young women and children board a liner on their way to Canada. Most would not return home until the end of the war.

The third wave

After the Blitz ended in May 1941, German bombing of British cities became less intense. The damage caused by German bombers was far less than anticipated. People got used to spending each night in an air-raid shelter and then emerging the next morning to carry on their daily lives. As a result, many evacuated children and adults returned home after 1942.

In the first four months of 1944, however, German bombers carried out a 'Baby' or 'Little' Blitz against London and other cities. New evacuation plans for schoolchildren were drawn up. Most Londoners, however, stayed at home, so very few children were evacuated. This situation changed dramatically after the first V-1 flying bomb fell on East London in June 1944. The V-1 – or 'doodlebug' as it was popularly known – was an unmanned missile carrying a 1-tonne warhead. The V-1 was not very accurate but caused immense damage across London and the southeast of England.

A V-1 flying bomb lands in London during the Baby Blitz; these bombs prompted many people to flee the capital for the safety of the countryside.

INSIDE STORY:

'There was a lull in the bombing and we came home; then the doodlebugs started coming over. I was so frightened … One came down near us – the plaster came off the walls – we were surrounded by broken glass. My uncle came round and said, "You've got to go away, you can't stay here!" We went to Gloucester again.'

Phyllis Wilkins remembers the V-1 attacks.

London children take shelter underground to protect themselves during an air-raid.

Within days of the first V-1 attack, many evacuees fled back to the countryside, while others left London for the first time. By the end of August 1944, 1.2 million people had left the capital by themselves, with another 275,000 people helped by the official evacuation schemes. Most people remained away until the end of the year, when they felt it was safe to return. They then started to come back at the rate of about 10,000 a week from January onwards, even though attacks by the V-1 – and the even more powerful V-2 rocket – continued until March 1945. By then, the official evacuation scheme had ended. It was clear that Britain was going to win the war.

Think about
Would you have stayed in London during the V-1 raids?

Going home

The return of evacuees to areas that had missed the V-weapon attacks, such as Birmingham and Manchester, began on 6 December 1944. In March 1945, evacuees began to return home to London and southeast England.

Most people returned home with great joy, as they would be reunited again with family and friends. Others had mixed feelings. They had had fitted in very well with their new families and made good friends away from home.

After the war was over, people began to consider whether evacuation had been worthwhile. The expected level of deaths from air-raids – once estimated at 66,000 deaths a week – was far less, with about 60,000 people losing their lives from air-raids throughout the entire war. Most children would have been just as safe if they had stayed at home and gone to an air-raid shelter during an attack. Evacuation cost a lot of money, £9 million from September 1939 to March 1940 alone, money that could have been spent on the war. Above all, evacuation caused a great deal of unhappiness by breaking up families and disrupting children's education.

A family emerge from their shelter to survey the wreckage of their house destroyed during an air-raid.

INSIDE STORY:

Here are two different views of evacuation. Rozel Garner said that in a lot of ways it was a good thing; *'I learnt a lot, I saw another side of life and got a wider outlook.'* Phyllis Wilkins disagreed: *'I regret that time; it was a waste. My education could have been better. I just feel I could have made more of myself.'*

However, evacuation did save lives. It also showed that the government cared about those affected by the bombing, and helped them keep their spirits up by taking their children to safety. Evacuation had a huge impact on society. It gave poor children a better life in the country, and showed wealthier people how tough life was for poor people in the cities. After the war, the government made great efforts to get rid of poor housing and improve the lives of working people.

Think about
Do you think evacuation was a good or a bad thing?

The end of the war saw great celebrations as troops returned home from service overseas and families were reunited and could return to their own homes.

Timeline

■ 1931	Government committee looks into ARP plans and produces first estimates of casualties.
■ 1935	ARP services extended from London to the whole of the country.
■ June–August 1938	Evacuation rehearsals in London and Birmingham.
■ September 1938	Germany threatens Sudetenland border area of Czechoslovakia, prompting fears of war in Britain; mass evacuation plans drawn up but are called off as agreement is reached with Germany at Munich.
■ 2 December 1938	First *Kindertransport* of 200 children arrives at Harwich from Berlin.
■ 1-3 September 1939	Germany invades Poland; Britain declares war on Germany at the start of World War II. Evacuation of London begins.
■ 10 May 1940	Winston Churchill becomes prime minister; Germany invades the Low Countries and France; second mass evacuation begins.
■ 20–28 June 1940	Evacuation of the Channel Islands.
■ July 1940–July 1941	Large numbers evacuated from Gibraltar.
■ 10 July–12 October 1940	Battle of Britain is fought between the RAF and *Luftwaffe*.
■ 7 September 1940	The Blitz begins when German bombers raid London.
■ 11 May 1941	The Blitz ends with a massive raid on London.
■ 7 December 1941	Japan attacks US forces at Pearl Harbor; USA joins war on Allied side, turning the war into a truly world war.
■ 21 January–19 April 1944	The 'Baby Blitz'.
■ 8 September 1944	Official evacuation scheme ends.
■ 8 May 1945	VE Day – Victory in Europe Day – celebrates end of the war in Europe.

Glossary

Air-Raid Precautions (ARP) Measures taken to protect people and buildings against air-raids.

Allies Countries linked to another by treaty of friendship.

Anti-Semitism Extreme prejudice against Jewish people.

Billet Temporary accommodation provided for people evacuated out of towns and cities at risk from air-raids.

Blitz, the The campaign by the German *Luftwaffe* to bomb British cities.

Bomb Hollow shell containing an explosive, incendiary or other destructive substance.

Bomber Military aircraft specially built to carry and drop bombs on an enemy target.

Civilian A person whose work or family is mainly civil rather than military.

Compensation Money paid to a country (or a person) for loss or injury.

Evacuation Movement of people from danger to a place of relative safety.

High explosive A powerful bomb.

Luftwaffe German air force.

Nazi Party Extreme political party led by Adolf Hitler that ruled Germany from 1933 to 1945.

RAF Britain's Royal Air Force.

Reception areas Safe place in the countryside where people would be evacuated to from the cities.

Refuge A safe place.

Stirrup pump Hand-operated device used to pump water to fight a fire.

WVS Women's Voluntary Service.

Further information

Books to read

In the War: The Blitz by Simon Adams (Wayland, 2008)

In the War: Food and Rations by Peter Hicks (Wayland, 2008)

In the War: School Life by Peter Hicks (Wayland, 2008)

World War Two: The Home Front by Ann Kramer (Franklin Watts, 2006)

World War Two: Causes, Course and Consequences by Simon Adams (Franklin Watts, 2005)

World War Two: Woman and War by Ann Kramer (Franklin Watts, 2005)

Eyewitness World War II by Simon Adams (Dorling Kindersley, 2004)

Websites

www.bbc.co.uk/history/worldwars/wwtwo
BBC history site.

www.worldwar2exraf.co.uk/Online%20Museum/ Museum%20Docs/Theblitz.html
Detailed site on the Blitz.

Note to parents and teachers: Every effort has been made by the publishers to ensure that these websites are suitable for children. However, because of the nature of the Internet, it is impossible to guarantee that the contents of these sites will not be altered. We strongly advise that Internet access is supervised by a responsible adult.

Index

Numbers in **bold** refer to pictures and captions.